A Small Still Voice

Torn Curtain Publishing
Wellington, New Zealand
www.torncurtainpublishing.com

© Copyright 2020 Diane Turner. All rights reserved.

ISBN Softcover 978-0-473-54821-6
ISBN EPub 978-0-473-54822-3

No portion of this book may be reproduced, stored in a retrieval system or transmitted in any form or by any means—electronic, mechanical, photocopy, recording or otherwise—except for brief quotations in printed reviews of promotion, without prior written permission from the author.

These are my memories and recollections of this journey. Other people's recollections of the same events may differ from mine.

Song lyrics from 'Girl on the Kitchen Floor' by Juliagrace are from the album Juliagrace: 'Girl on the Kitchen Floor,' 2016 Juliagrace. All rights reserved. Used by kind permission of Juliagrace.

Unless otherwise indicated, all Scripture quotations are taken from The Holy Bible, New International Version©, NIV©. Copyright© 1973, 1978, 1984, 2011 by Biblica, Inc. © Used by permission. All rights reserved worldwide. Scripture quotations marked TPT are from The Psalms: Poetry on Fire, The Passion Translation©, copyright © 2014. Used by permission of BroadStreet Publishing Group, LLC, Racine, Wisconsin, USA. All rights reserved. Scripture quotations marked The Message are taken from THE MESSAGE. Copyright © 1993, 1994, 1995, 1996, 2000, 2001, 2002. Used by permission of NavPress Publishing Group. Scripture quotations marked NLT are taken from the Holy Bible New Living Translation, copyright 1996, 2004, 2007, 2015 by Tyndale House Foundation. Used by permission of Tyndale House Publishers, Inc., Carol Stream, Illinois 60188. All rights reserved.

A record of this book is held at the National Library of New Zealand

A Small Still Voice

A collection of memories and reflections from a mother's heart on her journey through stillbirth and beyond

Diane Turner

For Lee, who has shared the whole journey with me.
And for our family,
Adam, Laura, Eitan & Xavier
Hannah & Mark
and Isaac.
I love you

Also, in loving memory of Reuben, baby Rosebud,
& the precious children
we hold in our hearts, not our arms.

From the Author

We all have stories to tell—happy, funny, sad. We live them; they make up the fabric of our lives. Sometimes we share them with our friends and families, and with those we come into contact with each day. Sometimes we choose to write our stories down and let others read them.

This is a small collection of my stories—memories, reflections and poems written over a number of years that I have chosen to share—which open up some of the 'Reuben-shaped' places in my life. Reuben was our baby who died before he had a chance to live his life.

To our children

Reuben would have been a young adult as I again attempt to gather my written reflections of this journey in his honour. There is no great sadness as I think about this—rather, a sense of wonder that the years have gone so fast.

Adam, Hannah and Isaac, I hope this book will invite you into a part of our lives you really don't know much about.

Adam, you may have some hazy memories of coming to the hospital with Nana Alison, of poking your baby brother and then finding it far more satisfying to run in and out of the curtains around my hospital bed. You may also remember coming into a room at home many, many times, looking at us and saying in a very matter of fact way, "Mum and Dad are crying again."

Hannah and Isaac, as Reuben's younger siblings, your only knowledge of your brother is from our photos and conversations. On days when you love life, be grateful to him. If Reuben had lived, it is unlikely we would have had any more children, so in a way your lives are the gift that arose from his death.

& to my readers

It surprises me how many people there are, even within my small circle of friends, who have suffered the loss of a child. Those I have spoken with all agree they would like to offer hope to others as a result of their experience. Nothing we go through is ever wasted if it can be used to help someone else.

Perhaps my writing can bring hope to someone who loses a baby or young child? Eventually, life does go on. Its shape changes, certainly—in fact, it can be pretty pear-shaped for a while—but it does not have to remain dark and empty forever. I found that, with time, life can be full of meaning and enjoyment, love, hope and laughter again.

I have written out of love for my family, for the child we lost, and for anyone reading who is experiencing their own heartache, sorrow, or grief. I have written in the hope my story will touch the hearts of those who read it. May the sharing of myself be a gift to you.

Beloved

You have called me your beloved.
As a mother gazes at her new-born baby
so you gaze at me
with such love and tenderness
it takes my breath away.

How amazing
and almost unbelievable
that You who are above all things
would feel like this about me—
that I am your beloved.

What response could I possibly make
with this incredible knowledge
of how much you love me,
a miracle of your creation,
but to call you beloved in return?

The miracle of normal

For you created my inmost being; you knit me together in my mother's womb. I praise you because I am fearfully and wonderfully made; your works are wonderful, I know that full well.
Psalm 139:13-14

It happens all the time—4.3 times every second, to be precise. And because it is so common, we tend to take it for granted. *What am I talking about?* It's the birth of a baby.

Generally speaking, we rejoice when our child is born. Often, we have dreamed of and planned for their arrival for months, or even years. But recognising the miracle, the 'gift' that our baby was conceived and formed in the womb, journeyed through the birth process and was delivered perfect? No, we don't usually stop, and marvel, and give thanks . . . because it's simply what we expect. It's normal.

I know from experience that our expectations are not always met.

Our baby was born dead.

He died somewhere between my bedtime one night, when he was very much alive and kicking, and early the next morning when I awoke. He was ready to be born, but passed away before he had a chance to live outside of my body.

A living baby is the norm, and I had expected to give birth to a healthy baby. Anything less had not crossed my mind. After all, I conceived easily, had enjoyed relatively easy pregnancies, and already had one healthy young son.

All the same, our baby—our beautiful, perfectly-formed baby with masses of dark hair, was born dead.

And as much as I wished this was only a bad dream, it quickly became our real-life nightmare.

Baby number one

Baby number one, Adam, gorgeous wee man!
Born according to our plan.
After all, that's what happens, isn't it?
Plan a baby, conceive a baby, birth a baby.
Healthy, happy ever after.

Baby number two.
Four months in the growing,
before we even knew.
Gone in another five,
our innocence gone with him.

Many of the parents we knew had 'baby number one' exactly as planned and never considered it would be any different in the future. We had healthy normal babies.

But just as childhood experiences can strip us of our innocence, early parenthood soon opened our eyes to previously unconsidered possibilities when many of our friends encountered difficulties the second time around—failure to conceive, miscarriage, stillbirth, babies born with life-threatening conditions, cot death . . .

Perhaps you can identify with, or even add to, this list.

Life is full of surprises and circumstances that we do not anticipate, but instead grow into—and through. Thankfully, many of these are good! But some are not.

Lord, keep our hearts soft and open to receive your love and consolation as we journey through this life with all its ups and downs. Open our eyes to see those with whom we can share our sorrows and those to whom we can pass on your comfort and unfailing love.

In the beginning

It's funny how easy it was. Getting pregnant, that is. And the way a routine doctor's visit can take an unexpected turn.

I was at an appointment for my young son, Adam, when I mentioned to the doctor that my body had not returned to its normal patterns since his birth. What should I do? We did want to try for another baby soon.

My wise doctor replied, "I'll do a pregnancy test first just in case," then pushed my tummy around a bit before promptly announcing, "You're about sixteen weeks pregnant!"

Actually, it was eighteen weeks.

How had I missed the obvious?!

I had presumed that regular aerobics classes were finally firming up my tummy muscles after Adam's birth, and that running around after a toddler was causing my tiredness. Even when a workmate had recently asked, "Are you pregnant?" my emphatic reply was, "No!"

"Well, for goodness sake, pull your tummy in then," she had said. *Ouch!*

How slow I was to not figure it out even with all those signs!

So, this was going to be a 'short' pregnancy. I developed morning sickness as soon as I knew I was pregnant even though I was already past the first twelve weeks when sickness is most common. It's fascinating how the mind and body work together. In any case, I have only a few distinct memories from that time.

I remember my mother telling people how large I was, and one of her friends seeing me and saying she didn't think so. *Hey, thanks Mum!*

I also remember having terrible leg pain as our baby pressed on my sciatic nerve during the last month or so. As far as I was concerned, this baby couldn't be born soon enough!

But there was an up-side to this pregnancy. One thing I am thankful for was that we never had to decide when we would try for a baby, nor agonise over the waiting. A blessing with each of our children was that falling pregnant was very easy.

Thank you, Lord, for the blessings, both noticed and unnoticed, that you send our way each day. I am very grateful.

This is the day!

It was more tiring to spend a whole day at home with twenty-month-old Adam than being at work, so I continued to work part-time, and gratefully let our mums share in his care right up until the day of Reuben's birth.

The due date for his birth came and went without any sign of labour.

It was the 29th April and I was more than a bit fed up. I was now forty-one weeks pregnant—a week overdue. Surely my wait would not be much longer! I left work early and drove home for a rest before collecting Adam from his grandparents.

That evening our midwife phoned to instruct me that, as she had a course to attend the next day, I was not to have our baby just yet! I jokingly agreed, and went to bed with a very active baby kicking around.

About midnight, however, I woke to find my waters had broken. Finally, I was in labour! I woke Lee up and remember being so glad that although our baby was overdue, he or she would still be born in April.

Lee had the fun job of washing the sheets, which we noticed were a little bloody, although we didn't realise something might be wrong. I had a bath and shaved my legs—or as much of them as I could reach—not knowing when I might have another opportunity.

At first, we delayed ringing the midwife, mindful of her earlier message, and because my previous labour had been extremely long. But eventually we made the call. Soon she arrived, and after a chat she examined me and listened for our baby's heartbeat. This took the longest time. She asked me some questions but apart from that, was rather quiet. I didn't think anything of it . . . until she said, very gently, "I can't find a heartbeat. It is possible that your baby is dead. Let's go to the hospital and check everything out."

She then went outside where we could not overhear the conversation and rang our doctor, I think to tell him that our baby was dead. Thankfully, my midwife knew that to introduce us to that possibility slowly and kindly was the best approach.

From then on everything became a blur. Lee's mum arrived to look after Adam and assured us all would be fine. Then we drove to the hospital to meet our doctor.

That's when it was confirmed. Our baby had died.

By now, strong labour pains had begun, each one a cruel reminder of what was yet to come; we had the whole birth process to go through for what now seemed no purpose at all. Ironically, I had been quite apprehensive for some time about having a 'normal' birth (Adam was born by caesarean section). Now, our 'normal birth' was not going to be so normal after all.

We settled in as best we could, waiting for our baby to be born. It was a quiet night in the delivery suite, and we had kind nurses popping in regularly to check on us. Gently they spoke of a new set of decisions we now needed to make—not how to cope with lack of sleep and two little ones, but would we like to see, hold . . . or even take our new baby home? We were given thoughtful warnings about how Reuben might look when he was born, as he had been dead for some hours.

Lee had the terrible task of calling our parents to tell them what had happened.

On reflection, it was a blessing to have had six hours of labour to process some of what lay ahead rather than receive the shocking news our baby was dead once he was born. At first, for example, when asked if I would like to hold our baby after he arrived, I found the idea rather repulsive. I had never seen a dead person before.

But by the time Reuben was born, around six-thirty the following morning, holding him seemed the natural thing to do.

I gave birth to an 8lb 14oz (4.045 kg) son. We named him Reuben Paul.

I don't know what I had subconsciously imagined, but I kept repeating that Reuben looked like a 'real' baby. He was the biggest of our babies, with a mop of dark hair and a long chubby body with no physical deformities. This made it much easier for us. He looked perfect.

Cuddling Reuben was no problem. Letting go of him was unbearably hard. And leaving him in the hospital when we went home was even harder; so ghastly that I cry even now as I remember it. Some weeks later I wrote a brief note enclosing the birth notice to our out-of-town friends.

It simply read:

> **TURNER-** Diane, Lee and Adam welcome with love Reuben Paul (stillborn), on Thursday, April 30, 1992 at Palmerston North Maternity Hospital. Our special thanks to Heather and John.

The Cry

This song is for the girl who had given up hope, who had watched her dreams and promises go up in smoke.
—Juliagrace

I remember the heart-rending cry. It was a sound of such deep distress, almost animal-like, and so loud it filled the room and beyond. I'm sure it penetrated the entire delivery suite. It was a scary sound and it took a moment to realise it was coming from me. It came from somewhere within the depths of my soul—the sound of the anguish of my physical pain, worse than anything I had experienced before as my baby was being pulled from my body with forceps, coupled with my emotional pain. Raw expressed honesty.

"Let it all out," said my midwife.

No way!

Once I knew I had made this terrible sound I shut my mouth firmly. I needed control. What if I couldn't stop screaming?

Looking back, I know that releasing my pain in this way would have been the healthy option. It took some grim determination to keep quiet. Funny what lengths I would go to in order to retain my control and dignity when the situation was outside of my control. And what on earth did dignity matter?

Much later I read the words of Isaiah 42:14: "For a long time I have kept silent, I have been quiet and held myself back. But now, like a woman in childbirth, I cry out . . ."

It was normal to cry out. Keeping quiet and holding back as I did was not God's intention for me or anyone else in distress or pain.

So, God, for all the cries I have stifled, for all the times I have not called out to you in my anguish, forgive me. Would you restore and heal me in those places where untended wounds still fester, where love lies bleeding? Break down any barricades I have erected and let your living cleansing water flow in me and through me. I long to be all you created me to be.

The care

*The light shines in the darkness, and the darkness
has not overcome it.*
John 1:5

Our hospital stay was marked by kindness. Such thoughtful loving kindness as others gave of themselves for us.

I think of the kind man from *Sands* (Stillbirth and Neonatal Death Support) who came to the hospital so early in the morning to take photos of our precious Reuben. He talked briefly and gently with us; he too had experienced a stillbirth. The photos were offered to us as a loving gift that we could keep and look at when and if the time was right. The precious memories he recorded may otherwise have been lost.

And there were other mementoes—the locks of Reuben's hair, and the wee thumb and footprint stamped for us. Then there were the rosebuds nurses picked from the hospital garden outside my window and placed on the pillow beside Reuben, the pretty gown they brought for him, the bedclothes for his tiny bed—all to make this sad room into a place of beauty and to ease our pain as best they could. To show us they cared.

Our parents and close friends visited. It was so important to us to have others meet and 'know' Reuben with us.

And then there was darling twenty-month old Adam who soon tired of inspecting and poking his unresponsive brother, preferring to dart in and out of the curtains around my bed and laugh with delight instead. To give us some breathing space and let our new reality begin to sink in, Lee's parents kindly took Adam to their home that night, but in the meantime, a moment of normality had been brought by a fun-loving child in the midst of great sadness. His was the only laughter to be heard in our family for some time.

Love gives. We were and are grateful.

Empty arms

Empty arms

Aching, empty arms

Being wheeled out of the maternity ward

in a wheelchair

without a baby.

Hearing the sound of babies

as we travel down the corridor

The longest walk

without a baby.

This is not how it is meant to be.

Tears streaming

Hearts breaking

Empty arms

Aching, empty arms.

The following day, we spent the morning cuddling our beautiful baby Reuben, counting his fingers and toes, measuring how long he was, being surprised by his mass of dark hair (our first son, Adam, was born with just a little, very fair hair).

How cold he was, poor wee man; his lips were blue instead of a healthy red.

We tried desperately to commit every detail to memory.

That afternoon, we returned home from hospital to a house full of flowers. Mum later told me this was Dad's way of showing love amidst his feelings of helplessness. How awful not to be able to fix your children's broken hearts!

Dad's story

At my request, my dear Dad bravely wrote of how he and Mum had experienced Reuben's birth. As I read, I realised their primary concern was for Lee and I, their children. Thanks, Dad! You and Mum were an amazing support team. I don't think there was anything you could have done better to help us.

My Dad wrote,

Medical misadventure . . . Was it caused by nurses or doctors? Was it God's fault? What can we do right now to help? Why? These were my immediate thoughts when Lee phoned from the maternity ward in the dark early hours of a Thursday morning to tell us our unborn grandson had died. That Diane would have to give birth normally/naturally to this dead child.

We were shocked and started to organise our thoughts. First and foremost, prayers for the Lord's comfort for the parents, for the safety of Diane, for the birth still to happen. No more sleep for us. We had to be with Lee at the hospital. Almost blind panic, being overcome by sensibility (dress warmly, drive sanely) . . . what would we expect or feel on seeing them? Feelings of desperation for them, self-pity for ourselves, prayers and more prayers.

When we arrived at the maternity room Reuben had been born and dressed. I felt relief that Diane was safe and well physically, but what about mentally, emotionally?

Lee was holding Reuben and offered us the chance of holding him. I was nervous and frightened by this, but eventually held this precious bundle who had long black hair, long fingernails. This was my only physical contact with my grandson Reuben, and the memory will live through the remainder of my life. I left that room feeling utterly shattered and broken. Not all for me, but mainly for Diane, Lee, Adam. I could not visualise the huge effect it would have on the parents . . . I believe strongly this death has shaped the path of Diane's search for more and more knowledge of Jesus and his work.

We came home and shared our thoughts. I wanted to fill her house with flowers. Joy. Celebration, not grieving. But celebration for what? Diane's health, Reuben's death? It was hard to know how to act. How did Lee and Diane feel? What could we as loving parents do, other than show love, help financially? We did several things, kept our total families together, shared meals, prayed.

Looking back now, did we think to find out Diane and Lee's feelings? We assumed we were helping, but I wouldn't know how to react very differently now if a similar incident occurred.

I would offer prayer, love, comfort, company still, but maybe a greater understanding of how the parents felt would help more.

Well, Dad, I don't know if we could have articulated our feelings in any useful way to you at that time. We were too shocked and numb to think clearly or intelligently. You and

Mum did a brilliant job of loving us through our grief—anticipating practical needs like food, finances, flowers, help with Adam . . . and your quiet presence, so we could talk when we wanted to about Reuben. These were all precious gifts. Thank you for sharing our journey.

We love you.

The days after

This song is for the girl with the tearstained face.
—Juliagrace

It was such an odd time to go clothes shopping. Reuben and I should have been resting and bonding with Lee and Adam and our families visiting us. After all, Reuben was born on Thursday and this was Friday.

But Reuben was dead and his funeral was to be held on Saturday.

My mother took me shopping to buy two outfits—something new for me that would fit my swollen body. And something new for Reuben. New outfits to dress us for his funeral.

It seemed there was so much to do amidst all the visitors—most importantly, we needed to plan a funeral. How do you do that in pain, numbness, confusion, never having done it before? And for our child, not our parent?

How do you do that with a body that has just given birth, a body that is tired and sore, torn from the birth process, breasts preparing to nurture a baby . . ?

Thank God for those who took over, took charge—our loving families.

We visited Reuben at the funeral home, dressed him in his new clothes and placed special, never to be played with, toys in his tiny coffin with him. We cuddled him so tight but then had to put him back down and leave, the ache growing larger not smaller with the cuddling. And then there were the funeral directors taking three attempts before they finally spelled 'Reuben' correctly. Didn't they know this was our child and his name was important?

Well-meaning visitors came but talked about everything except the reason they had come. Others were so uncomfortable that all my energy went into comforting them.

There were so many little indignities, sparking anger I could not voice. Like the morning of Reuben's funeral, as I was cleaning the toilet and tidying up, because that afternoon, people would be coming to our home. Or the family friend who sat in my lounge talking on and on without noticing me, while I stayed standing because there was nowhere to sit, even though my body felt ready to collapse.

Then there was such great thoughtfulness—cards, flowers, helpful loving visitors, people dealing with the practicalities of the funeral service and afternoon tea. My Godfather chose the perfect music to play for us at the funeral, and we sang along as best we could to, "All things Bright and Beautiful."

A workmate brought huge quantities of home baking to feed our guests. Others spent the whole afternoon in our kitchen dealing with food, drinks and cleaning up.

There was so much sorrow that day—especially walking out of the church after the funeral service—just Lee, Adam and I, with Lee carrying Reuben in his tiny coffin. Yet lighter moments interspersed the service. I vividly remember Adam looking at the Anglican priest in her white robes and excitedly telling us, "Look there's Jesus!"

Yes, Jesus. I'm sure you were very present with us in that place.

Remembering Reuben

When we visited the local cemetery, there were more decisions to make. Where was Reuben's memorial plaque to go? There was no special garden at that time for stillborn babies.

My parents suggested a spot which received full sun. That seemed as good as any to us.

The next decision was what to put on the plaque remembering Reuben? We wandered around to get ideas. As we walked through the children's cemetery looking at other people's memorials, we realised we were one family among many who had lost children. We even knew some of the families represented there but had not known that part of their story. In the end, we chose as the inscription:

Reuben Paul Turner
Stillborn 30 April 1992
Safe in the arms of Jesus

These days we do not visit the cemetery very often. For me it is a place I can go to remember Reuben, but it is not the only place. I prefer to remember him wherever I am, especially at home, outdoors, at the beach, and at all places that are special to us as a family.

We do notice on our visits, however, that someone has often been there before us and that Reuben's little area is always well looked after and his plaque polished. We have asked around but haven't discovered who the caring person is. If it is you and you are reading this, thank you so much!

Night

This song is for the hearts who are shattered and torn, who are living in the darkest hour just before the dawn. Hold on, better days are coming.
—Juliagrace

The pain did not end after the funeral. In fact, it was night after night, long and dark, that the pain was at its worst, when I would awaken and remember in a sleepy haze, "Dead! Our baby is dead!"

I was hoping, clutching at straws, that this was all a terrible nightmare and that if I were awake it would be over. Reaching for my baby bump to check if it was real, I could only find . . . no baby bump.

Our baby *had* been born. Yes, this was indeed a terrible nightmare and we were living in it, through the long dark night and beyond.

Our Father, thank you that Lee and I had each other so that we did not have to face this worst of times alone. Thank you that in the darkest of nights we could reach out, cling to each other, love and comfort each other. Thank you that Lee let me grieve long and kept strong for me, delaying his own grieving process until I could better cope.

Pain

A jagged break

Splinters of fragmented glass

Piercing the space

Where your heart should be

A loss too hard to understand

Where there was once the promise

Of a life to be lived

Now nothing but memories

And silent emptiness

And then another break.

How could there be any more feeling left?

Yet these splinters have shattered further

And continue to wound

With a relentless stabbing pain

More broken dreams

What left to live for?

Sorrow, grief too deep to describe

Too hard to bear

Numbness to block out the hurt

Anger

Why? Why me?

Where is the fairness in life?

God? What God?

Where is He?

Why did He let this happen?

And exhaustion

From the sobbing

and constant emotional turmoil

In sleep the dreams come

What if it didn't really happen?

What if this is only a ghastly nightmare?

Waking to discover it is real

Heartbroken all over again

Of course, there are people

Those who don't want to know
And those who love and care
But they are not in your shoes
No one knows your heart
Your suffering, your life

Except for One
The same God of whom
you asked the questions
And maybe raged at

If above the turmoil and confusion
You can hear Him, He will say:
Come, give me what you have.
Yell at me, cry to me,
share your despair, your hopelessness.

I am holding you in everlasting arms
and will not drop you.
All I want from you
is to come as you are and be real
And know that I know everything about you.

I can feel your every breath mirrored in me
When you hurt, I hurt.

I want more than anything for you to let me in
to love you, to weep with you
to sit quietly with you,
to be your friend, comforter, restorer
and lover of your very soul.

I promise no instant cure
But over time I can heal you.
And, if you share your journey with me
There can be joy amidst the pain.

Do not ask to understand.
Just know that I am with you
Solid, strong, unchanging
Your lifeline.
And we can travel forward together
To a new place.

What to say?

In the midst of suffering no one needs clarifying arguments as much as they need to feel arms close.
—Ann Voskamp, The Broken Way[1]

People have often asked me, "What can we say that will help in a situation like that?"

I came to the conclusion after Reuben's death that there are no right words. Certainly, we received plenty of unhelpful comments like, "Never mind dear, you can have another one—and you've already got Adam," or, "It must be God's will," or, "God has a plan for your life." Others said, "Time will heal you," or remarked, "I know how you feel."

While some of those words may be true—and were presumably spoken with the best of intentions—they were simply not helpful. We did not need anyone to tell us they knew how we felt, to try and fix the unfixable or explain the unexplainable.

---

[1] 1. Ann Voskamp, The Broken Way (Grand Rapids, Zondervan, 2016), page 237

But more hurtful than thoughtless or inappropriate comments were those who ignored the situation. A few people acted as though our pregnancy and Reuben's birth and death had never happened. At the time, I was too bewildered and vulnerable to question their behaviour, and I don't think they were being deliberately harsh; they just did not know how to deal with us. A little discomfort on their part and acknowledgement of our loss would have been welcome. After all, we had not faced this before either.

The words that brought real comfort were honest and thoughtful. A heart tuned in to the hurting person brings words and actions which can help and heal. Maybe it's as simple as saying, "I'm sorry," or "I don't know what to say." Hugs, shared tears, expressions of loving concern, and simply being with us with no words, were all gratefully received. Someone giving me the opportunity to talk if I needed to while they listened, was also very helpful.

God, the Master of time, time does heal to a certain extent, doesn't it? Routines and the normal events of everyday life all help heal too. Thank you for the rhythms of our lives. Thank you especially for those who walk alongside us as we travel through the dark and difficult places.

Girl on the Kitchen Floor

The song by *Juliagrace*, 'Girl on the Kitchen Floor,' had me in floods of tears the first time I heard her sing it. I ached for the 'girl' I was back in those sad days when I cried, not on the concrete every night, but on the couch every day and in bed every night. Still, I heard truth and hope sung to me, that girl, through her lyrics . . .

> This song is for the girl on the kitchen floor
> I'm so grateful that I'm not her any more
> But I never will forget how she cried there
> on the concrete every night
>
> This song is for the girl who had given up hope
> Who had watched her dreams and promises
> go up in smoke
> As she faced the bitter knowledge
> that there was no more comfort in sight
> This song is for the girl with the tearstained face
> This song is for the hearts who are shattered and torn

Who are living in the darkest hour just before the dawn
Hold on. Better days are coming

I wanna tell that girl that life will be beautiful again
I wanna tell that girl that her days
will be full of love again
I've got miles and miles to go
But in my heart of hearts I know
There is so much left to live for
Girl on the kitchen floor

Thankfully those better days certainly did come.

God of Hope, give us courage to dare to hope in our places of despair and darkness. Speak into our hearts that life can be beautiful and full of love and that there is so much more to live for. Wrap us in your arms of love and comfort and speak tenderly to us as we lie on our kitchen floor. Bring healing and lift us to our feet again.

On we go

Returning to 'normal' life. How is that possible after a death? Normal for me now included a daily ritual of putting Adam down for his afternoon nap, then falling onto the couch to sob my heart out. It meant walking past Reuben's room, lovingly prepared but now with the door firmly shut and wondering when and how I might go in there again. What about packing everything away? It meant steeling myself when I opened the freezer in case I found more baby food I had prepared and frozen in advance.

Normal life meant coming to terms with a body healing too slowly, still painful and torn from giving birth—and the frustration of a body that didn't know there was no baby to feed and that no milk production was required.

'Normal' meant leaving the house—such a scary thought. At first, I told everyone I met that I had two children even though they only saw one. In retrospect, it must have seemed very strange to be given that information by a woman they didn't even know.

Being around other babies was hard to cope with, and at our stage of life there were lots of babies. A visitor who came to our weekly playgroup had a baby who weighed Reuben's exact birth weight. I pored over this wee one, exploring him and just drinking in all I could of a baby who was the same size as mine but, unlike mine, alive.

A week after Reuben was born there was a special occasion—one of my playgroup friends was expecting her second baby and had planned a home birth where we were all welcome to be present! When I was called and told her labour was underway, I couldn't bring myself to be there for the birth, and instead arrived soon after her baby boy was born. What an honour it was (and painfully healing) to be handed this precious bundle for a cuddle. His mum understood.

It was about three weeks after Reuben's birth when I returned to work. This was another unexpected change—the plan had been that I would take time to be at home with our new baby, but as there was no new baby, we decided my work life may as well continue as before. And so, going through the motions and feeling very empty inside, I resumed another part of my pre-Reuben life.

It's such a strange feeling to return to a place after everything has changed for you, only to find that nothing in that place has changed. I returned to work a different person and found it very difficult to listen to the inconsequential chatter at tea breaks. I understood other people's lives went on, but now their concerns seemed so trivial. Didn't they know there were huge things happening in my life?

I remember a couple of phone calls from my first few days back at work. One was with an unsuspecting young man who, on hearing I had been off work, asked if I had been on holiday. I replied tersely, "No, I had a baby," to which he responded, "Congratulations!" When I snapped back, "My baby died," he had no answer and ended the call as soon as he could.

Another conversation with a client who was a counsellor had a happier outcome as she knew how to respond and carry on a conversation after hearing my news, even offering her services if required.

Obviously, it was difficult for people to know how to act. My work family were very caring, very supportive, but in the end, everyone's lives went on and work continued.

Grief

This song is for the girl on the kitchen floor,
I'm so grateful that I'm not her anymore
but I never will forget how she cried
there on the concrete every night.
—Juliagrace

We all respond to our losses differently. For quite a while I had a routine time and place set aside to consciously grieve.

Because I had Adam to care for, much of my day was spent just getting on with it, doing the things mothers do. However, the time I was desperate for was after I put Adam to bed for his afternoon nap. Then I lay on the couch and cried my eyes out. Somehow after that I was able to pull myself together again until the next day. Knowing I would have this time to feel and express the pain of my broken heart helped me to keep going.

I was visited early on by another heartbroken mum who had lost her baby a week before Reuben. Her grief was still very raw, and I think our sharing was helpful to us both.

Our midwife also continued to visit us after Reuben's birth, just as she would have if he had been with us. She was a real support, someone who had shared our journey. And it was she who linked me up with another mum who had undergone a similar birth experience.

Another source of comfort, not only to me, but for my wider family, was Eric Clapton's song, "Tears in heaven," which my mum introduced me to. I was unaware of it at the time, but the song, which was written for his young son, was released around the time Reuben died. The lyrics made me think of my own son, and the grief he might have experienced in those hours before his birth. Later I wrote,

Reuben, I don't know if you suffered before you died I often wonder if you were kicking around so much that last night because there was something wrong. Were you hurting?

I am so grateful for the peace you received so soon after and for God's promise that He will wipe every tear from your eyes.

I attended a *Sands* meeting on my own soon after Reuben died as Lee did not want to come. I felt very vulnerable but hoped it would help me. The group wasn't right for me (possibly I wasn't ready for it) and I didn't go back. But that evening, I spoke to people who had suffered over and over again—multiple miscarriages and stillbirths—many of whom had no surviving children. I was so thankful we had Adam; our lot seemed so much better than theirs.

There was, however, a time about three months after Reuben died when I was so distraught that, unbeknownst to me, Lee called a friend to come and be with me after he had left for work. That friend came and cared and helped me get back on an even keel again.

It was a very dark time for us. The only thing we really felt would help would be another pregnancy, another baby.

I know this isn't the same for everyone who loses a child. At the time, I was corresponding with, and trying to encourage, another mum whose baby had died during birth. This mum was in so much pain I think to her having another baby would have seemed like a betrayal of the one she had just lost. When I eventually wrote that I was pregnant again, she did not reply, and our contact ended.

In the meantime, generous friends offered us the use of their timeshare near Melbourne, Australia, and my parents offered to pay our airfares so we could have a holiday. This was a precious gift, especially as Lee and I had never travelled overseas together. For us, getting away really helped—and it was on our return that we discovered I was pregnant again! Maybe life was improving!

Why?

Why, why, why, Lord?

Not why me

as opposed to someone else

I would not wish this on anyone else.

Just why?

Why? Why? Why? This was my constant cry for so long. There was nothing visibly wrong with my baby except that he was born dead. There was no answer to the question, 'Why?'

And yet eventually the 'why?' question stopped. Some would say this is what happens as time passes. I think God replaced the question with his peace which is beyond my understanding. I had no answer to the question . . . just a sense of not needing to know any more. Somehow the burning question was gone, replaced by a simple trust.

And when things in life go terribly wrong now, as they do, I do not ask the 'why' question.

God knows, God cares. And somehow that is enough.

Looking out of my kitchen window one morning I realised I was interested in what was going on in my garden. I was at peace.

Thank you, Lord, for using your beautiful creation to welcome me back into life!

The stillness

How I long to be in that place

Where there is just you

And me

And no-one else

And I can come and curl up

Without any words

With you

And you know

All there is to know

You gently begin to heal me

Pouring out your love with a touch

Offering words of encouragement

and understanding

Stirring my soul until I weep

And you weep with me

Tears sealing our bond

Until I am strong

With your strength

And I can leave our sanctuary

To face the day

With the knowledge

That I am not alone

And that you

Will welcome me back

As the most special one

When I choose to return

Glimpses of a new normal

I wanna tell that girl that life will be beautiful again.
—Juliagrace

Through my wonderful midwife I was introduced to a woman and her husband who had lost their second son in similar circumstances to ours and had since had two more children. I began calling on her once a week. The biggest blessing was being able to talk with someone who could relate to my experiences because they were often also hers. These mornings became a lifeline for me. Adam and I would sit in the living area as my new friend looked after her little ones.

Her normality was immensely reassuring. At times in my grief I felt as though maybe I was going crazy and, what if life was always going to be like this? Seeing her with her children, however, gave me the hope that one day I too could have more babies and a lovely complete family as she did.

Jen, I have so much to thank you for. You were such a huge part of my healing. What a gift to be able to come to your home week after week, have you patiently listen to me and understand because you had been there too. To look at your life, your family and see you were 'normal' even after losing a child gave me great hope for my family's future.

Thank you for being willing to let me in and share your mornings, especially as you were busy with a new baby, another little one and a child at school. You never caused me to feel I was an interruption or a nuisance although I am sure, at times, I was both.

Sharing your experience and your life with me was a truly priceless gift.

In the tapestry of life, Lord, our lives are interwoven by you with just the right people at just the right times. Thank you for my midwife and my new friend, especially the blessing of her being willing to open her heart and her home to me in the season of my great need.

Stronger

What doesn't kill you makes you stronger
Isn't that what we were taught when times got tough?

Strong?
Seems to me there are two types of strong.
You can steel yourself and stuff the pain
somewhere down deep, secure it tight
Barricaded in a deep dark cell
Never again to see the light of day

Out of sight out of mind,
Dealt with and now I can go on
Strong again, but numb
with a heart of stone

And somehow
That locked away pain
seeps out
Quietly leaks

Stains everything

rusty brown

With bitterness

With anger

With resentment

Hurting people hurt people

Stronger?

Or sapped of strength?

Strong?

Seems to me

there are two types of strong.

What if

I leave the pain be?

Acknowledge it

Endure it

Try not to be afraid of it

What if I allow myself

to be vulnerable?

To keep on feeling

as much as it hurts

for as long as it takes

And maybe my heart

will remain soft

Able to receive

the love and compassion

others offer

Able to heal

and pass on

the same comfort

that has been received

Stronger?

Yes

Scarred. But alive and well

Stronger.

With hope

and courage for the future.

New life

It was the day of another funeral. This time we were saying farewell to one of my mum's close friends. Mum was hurting that day.

I had chosen the day of the funeral to tell my parents of our new pregnancy, hoping to bring Mum good news as she grieved.

It's funny that as I reflect on this so many years later, I don't recall my visit to the doctor, getting confirmation I was pregnant, or even sharing the news with Lee.

I do remember the scariness of it all, the 'what ifs?' as we considered the future. What if it all happened again and this baby died too? Yet we desperately wanted another child, not to replace Reuben, but as part of rebuilding our life. This pregnancy was a risk we needed to take.

And I so badly needed to fall pregnant when I did. In this low patch about three months after Reuben's birth, I wondered if I was going mad. I don't know how long I could have continued in that state and thankfully did not need to find out.

For some reason Mum wasn't with us as we walked from the car to the funeral and so I told Dad I was expecting another baby. Cautiously he asked, "Is that good?" I hadn't even considered that response! Of course it was good!—though at the same time, terrifying.

Curiously, I don't remember telling my Mum the news—I only remember that I hoped to cheer her on this sad day, to be a blessing to her, not to give her another load to carry. In my mind at that time, another pregnancy could only be good news.

God, you live outside of time and yet you time the events of our lives perfectly. Thank you that you give good gifts. Thank you that I was able to conceive again so quickly, for the healing a new baby brought us. I thank you especially for the special gifts of Adam, Hannah and Isaac in our lives.

Joy

*I wanna tell that girl that her days will
be full of love again.*
—*Juliagrace*

And what good news it was! The pregnancy went smoothly—although my pregnancy with Reuben had also, so we knew this was no guarantee our baby would arrive safe and healthy.

Facing the possibility our new growing baby may also die, we realised the only time we may have together was while I was carrying him or her. It was important to know as much about this child as we could and to discover its sex at the first opportunity.

But this was not to be. My specialist scanned our baby very early on and then decided there was no need for a further scan as the pregnancy progressed. All we knew was that bubs was either a girl or a boy!

Throughout this pregnancy, on the one hand we dared not hope for a healthy baby. Yet on the other, God gave us hope stronger than our fear, so at the same time we prepared as anyone would—the room, the clothes—the anticipation and excitement tinged with anxiety, but expecting we would have a living baby to bring home with us this time.

Towards the end of my pregnancy, though I was regularly monitored at the hospital I became somewhat anxious. The birth was to be an elective caesarean at thirty-nine weeks, which gave me comfort both in knowing I only had to 'hold on' for a set time and that the birth would be relatively quick.

Reuben was born at forty-one weeks and had been alive and kicking the night I went into labour. At thirty-nine weeks he was definitely alive, and I focused on this thought while waiting for our new baby's arrival. I guess it's similar to someone who has experienced a miscarriage at twelve weeks feeling all is well after that time. Thirty-nine weeks felt like a very long time to wait for the danger period to be over.

We were treated with kindness at the hospital when the day arrived, and we were prepared for our baby's birth. I never knew an epidural injection to be so painful. I had had two previously, but these were both given during labour when the pain of my contractions had obviously been greater.

So, to the birth and the longed-for good news!

Our baby was alive and healthy. Thank you, Lord!

After the birth of two sons I thought of myself as a mother of boys, but surprise, surprise . . . this time we had been blessed with the most beautiful baby girl.

What joy! I have never been as elated as the night after Hannah was born. I kept her in bed with me for as long as possible; the pure joy I felt is not something I can describe. We had a new baby, a daughter who was alive and perfect.

It was less than a year after Reuben when Hannah was born. I cannot imagine how we would have coped with the first anniversary of his birth and death a few weeks later without Hannah to cuddle on that day. But God is good, and we cuddled our way through.

About two and a half years later, came the birth of our precious son, Isaac.

Once again we had to 'hold on' for thirty-nine weeks waiting for his birth, but with the comfort of knowing all had gone well with my previous pregnancy and birth.

We had no idea at the time, how much our new born son would enrich our lives. Or how much healing his birth would also bring. Carrying him was also an anxious time, but less so than with Hannah.

I was asked to write an article about our experience with Reuben and also to talk to a group of people who were studying grief. Both these activities were good therapy for me.

Early in my pregnancy we learned we were expecting a son, and I confided in my mother as I was unsure what my reaction would be to the birth of another boy. Would I expect him to be a 'replacement Reuben'? I was so relieved to find it was not like that at all!

I stayed in hospital with Isaac for five days after his birth and took such pleasure in getting to know this beautiful new baby of ours. With Isaac's arrival our family now seemed complete.

Psalm 30:5 says, "Weeping may last for the night, but . . . joy comes in the morning" (NASB).

It certainly did for us on the mornings Hannah and Isaac were born.

Those birth conversations

Something I feel I have missed out on (or maybe been cheated out of) is taking a full part in conversations with other mothers about their birth experiences.

I would sit and listen as other mums compared notes and laughter at the shared horror and blessing of it all. What could I say? *"I've had three caesareans, and my only 'normal' birth was spent waiting for my dead baby to be born. Want to hear about it?"* A bit of a conversation killer.

"It was painful in every way. Worst at the end when Reuben was finally delivered using forceps without any pain relief because the epidural had worn off. I can't begin to describe how painful that was; I've never felt anything like it before or since…

"Then for a couple of weeks afterwards the torn tissue was so sore while it healed. Along with overfull breasts that were swollen and aching even while taking tablets to dry up my milk."

Who knew to enquire or offer sympathy for these unseen problems? I was too vulnerable to offload them onto anyone else. So instead of putting a dampener on the discussions, I tended to keep quiet. Looking back, I could have explained my dilemma and that I would talk about my births if anyone wanted to listen. Some probably would have been happy to. Being different made me supersensitive, I guess.

Sometimes I did speak out of my hurting places when someone else was really moaning and feeling sorry for themselves.

Did it really matter if your birth experience did not match your plan? You wanted no pain relief, but you ended up taking some? You wanted a home birth but ended up in hospital? Actually, as long as you and your baby were both healthy and alive then the rest was not so important.

It was kind of unfair to dump my stuff on them, but I hope I also offered a different perspective for them to consider. Gently encouraging a mum with an unfortunate birth experience or miscarriage to tell her story and then taking the time to listen well, I believe, is thoughtful and kind. I would have liked someone to do this for me.

Lord, the hurting manifests in lots of different ways and at unexpected times. Continue to pour your healing balm into the depths of the wound. Give me courage to speak out when that would help. And take away the bitterness so anything spoken would be with love and gentleness.

Where are you, God?

And I am convinced that nothing can ever separate us from God's love. Neither death nor life, neither angels nor demons, neither our fears for today nor our worries about tomorrow—not even the powers of hell can separate us from God's love. No power in the sky above or in the earth below—indeed, nothing in all creation will ever be able to separate us from the love of God that is revealed in Christ Jesus our Lord.

Romans 8: 38-39 (NLT)

A few years after Reuben's birth, I believe God prompted me to write about where *He* was in our journey through Reuben's birth and death. The following paragraphs are taken from the beginning and end of that piece of writing . . .

There are so many events in this world that are bad on a global scale and at a personal level. I believe it is helpful for us to know where we think God is when a crisis strikes. If we can see where He has been in the past, then we may know where to look for Him in our next time of need and to do so with trust and hope.

To be excitedly preparing for the birth of our second child one day and planning his funeral the next was devastating. I have been aware God was at work in so many ways as He nursed us through and beyond that experience. I believe He set the foundations way back when Lee and I were born into loving, supportive families. We have also been blessed with good caring friends. And we knew each other well, having been married for ten years when Reuben was born. The death of a child can more often break a marriage relationship than strengthen it, so our existing relationship being strong was important for our future together . . .

What have I learned from all this?

I would like to think I have grown in my understanding of, and compassion for, other people in their suffering.

I would also like to be able to say I am now a model wife and mother, with my priorities always being God first, then family and then everything else. Of course, I am not a model anything and my priorities are often way off the mark.

However, I do remember and often marvel anew at how precious and fragile the gift of life is. And with this knowledge comes a reassessment of the way I am living mine.

I do know where God is when 'bad things' happen to me.

He is right there sharing every step of my journey. God has promised me (and you) that He will never leave us. God prepared the way for us before our 'bad thing' happened. He smoothed the way and set the right relationships in place to bring us through our suffering stronger than before, holding us always in His everlasting arms. And I know that there is nothing that can come our way that we cannot deal with as long as we rely on Him.

> All praise and glory to our God!
>
> He weeps with us
>
> He carries us through
>
> He does not hurry us for He has all the time it takes
>
> He gives us hope
>
> He has suffered
>
> His grace, mercy and compassion are endless
>
> And He is glorious
>
> This is our God
>
> All praise to our awesome God
>
> All glory and honour to You who reign on high
>
> And walk below with us

Twenty-one today

The 30th April was approaching again, only this year, Reuben would have been turning twenty-one. And whereas his anniversary hadn't been a big deal for me for some years, I kept thinking about this one as it approached.

When the day arrived, I couldn't face going to work. My understanding boss said, "That's fine. See you tomorrow." I wasn't distraught, but simply needed some time to reflect and remember.

I looked through some photos taken at the hospital and funeral home prior to Reuben's funeral. Lee and I looked so young back then.

Reuben's picture was already etched in my memory. He was beautiful in our eyes, but his skin colour was mottled and his lips were blue at birth so he may not have appeared so attractive to other people.

Thumbing through photos of us cuddling him tightly in the funeral home brought tears as I remembered our last goodbye hugs.

I reread the funeral service. What a blessing! For a simple service, the words were profound and beautiful. At the time I doubt I heard them, but the truth of God's love and care and His promises were such a comfort and joy on this Memorial Day.

I took a long walk by the river and then met special friends for lunch, so grateful that our regular lunch date fell on this day.

Later I wrote Reuben a letter—something I wanted to do even though it felt rather odd—and while I was sad that there were joys in life he would never experience, I was also grateful for the heartaches and trials he would not have to endure.

The bottom line, he is with God, 'safe in the arms of Jesus' as his plaque at the cemetery reminds us, and I cannot imagine the bliss for him in that life which is his.

He has begun ". . . chapter one of the Great Story which no one on Earth has read: which goes on for ever: in which every chapter is better than the one before."[2]

---

[2] 2. C. S. Lewis, The Last Battle (1956, The Bodley Head; repr., Puffin Books, 1968), page 165

Reuben's Birthday Letter

What would I say to you today, Reuben? Twenty-one today! Happy, happy birthday.

If you followed the normal path, then those late teenage years could have been ones of pulling away, making a statement of independence, learning to stand on your own two feet . . .

Hopefully you might have avoided the drinking culture and cut straight to the 'lovely young man' stage. Full of life and energy. Would there be a young woman on the scene? Would you be handsome, tall, short, wide, thin? A musician, student, sportsman like your brothers, dreamer, thinker?

There are joys and milestones you will never experience—particularly relationships with friends and family, love, marriage, children . . . and there are heartaches, also related to those same relationships—love, marriage and children. Reuben, I am so glad you have been spared the heartache.

I wonder what you think and feel as you look down on us, if you do . . .

You know God is real and you can see and experience His love, Father to son—it's all you've known except for nine brief months.

Reuben, I hope your death was peaceful, not turbulent. You were so loved and wanted . . .

And yet, your passing allowed us the gift of Hannah and Isaac.

Your 'life' is not one we can comprehend. And, I hope to meet you one day; in fact, my hope is that all the family will, and maybe some already have? I hope we will know each other, be able to talk and laugh and I know that we will love, because God is love.

Reuben, twenty-one years ago God blessed us and He blessed you. We love you. Happy birthday!

Loving God, You have ordained the number of days each of us have here on this earth. So, for whatever reason, Reuben's short life in utero only was no accident. I trust Your perfect plan for his life Lord and thank you his eternity with You has begun.

From a distance

In my heart of hearts I know, there is so much more to live for.
—*Juliagrace*

Looking back many years on, the strange thing is, although the awfulness of living through and coming to terms with the loss of Reuben cannot really be described, I wouldn't choose to change it.

No, I would never have wished for this to happen and I would love Reuben to be with us. But our experience has shaped and deepened us in ways no other situation could.

Suffering does that. You dig deep into reserves you did not know you possessed. It takes grit and determination and just clinging on by your fingernails sometimes, but there is, by God's grace, enough strength for the journey.

We had an opportunity to see the goodness in people as so many came alongside to help us get through. And each person's help was unique—some practical, like providing food or taking over chores; some personal . . . gifts given, notes penned, speaking the right word at the right time, encouraging, hugging and sharing tears; some quietly unnoticed in the background, offering up prayers or supporting those who were supporting us.

Suffering is part of life. If we can embrace it rather than trying to push it away, we can grow through it. Nothing is ever wasted. What we have learned and become through this time has, I believe, enabled us to better understand and help others in need.

I am grateful to have had the time and opportunity to reflect on the years since Reuben was born. It is both satisfying and fulfilling to re-read my stories and gather them together.

I notice that as time has passed, my raw emotions have healed and I may not have always written in the feelings of the moment. But I have always written from my heart.

I started to write hoping others who have suffered loss may be able to relate to something of mine, to receive comfort and a glimmer of hope that their lives can also be good again.

Along the way I also realised I wanted our children to have the opportunity to know about this part of me. For while this has been a shared journey with my husband Lee, what I have written is essentially expressing my own heart.

More recently I have persevered because I had a sense that if left unfinished, this 'labour of love' would be like another stillbirth. I do not want that. So I have endeavoured to complete my Reuben story and trust God it will be read by those it is meant to bless.

Beauty for ashes

Blessed are those whose strength is in you,
whose hearts are set on pilgrimage.
As they pass through the Valley of Baka (weeping)
they make it a place of springs.
Psalm 84:5-6a (parentheses mine)

This was a cry from my heart early on in this journey. It has been answered.

You, Lord, are the God who has promised us beauty in exchange for ashes. We come to you broken with nothing to give but our emptiness, our hopelessness. The burnt remains of our hopes, our dreams, our lives. In your great compassion and mercy, we ask that you hold us tenderly. Comfort and restore us. Resurrect our lives. We long to have hope and joy again in you, through you, because of you. Lord, hear our prayer. To you be the glory for ever and ever.

A good Father

Only God is my Saviour, and He will not fail me.
Psalm 62:5b (TPT)

Today as I was reading, I was struck by the words, "I lifted him like a baby to my cheek . . ." (Hosea 11:4 MSG)

I remembered the wonder of lifting a little one and feeling a soft face next to mine, hearing each breath, the closeness and delight and intimacy of those special moments.

I thought about the love a parent has for their child, a gift so precious, and especially the love of a father for his child. A photo of Lee holding Reuben came to mind. He was hugging him so tightly yet gently in his grief, loving, hurting, not wanting to let go.

If we, created in God's image, feel like this then I wonder how much greater is God's love for us? How much more delight does He take in tenderly lifting and holding and caring for us? How much more pain does He feel when we hurt?

Psalm 23:1 in the Passion Translation says, "The Lord is my Fierce Protector and my Pastor."

Thinking of that photo of Lee with Reuben helps me to see and believe this and to trust God more with myself and my life and also with those who are precious to me. How much safer they are in His care!

As I remember Reuben, permanently in His care and presence, I smile and say,

Thank you, God.

You are a good, good Father.

Thank you

May the God of hope fill you with all joy and peace as you trust in him, so that you may overflow with hope by the power of the Holy Spirit.
Romans 15:13

My grateful thanks to all who have shared and continue to share this journey with Lee and I, especially our parents without whom we may not have made it through the early days.

Also to those generous friends who have encouraged me with my writing and, more recently, those who have helped in the painful process of putting it all together. Without your love, prayers and practical support *'A small, still voice'* may never have been completed.

To those who have taken the time to read *'A small, still voice'* and have perhaps also passed it on to someone else to read, thank you for sharing in my story.

May God continue to bless you all so that you may continue to pass on His blessings.

And to God, Father, Son and Holy Spirit, who has raised me up and brought me to life, thank you for your unfailing love and faithfulness. Thank you for new mercies each morning and your strength which has carried me especially in my weakest moments. Thank you for your grace, for guiding me and for bringing light into the dark places. Thank you for your beautiful creation which continually brings joy to my soul.

To You be the glory.

To get in touch with Diane, please email:

dmaree5001@gmail.com

www.ingramcontent.com/pod-product-compliance
Ingram Content Group UK Ltd.
Pitfield, Milton Keynes, MK11 3LW, UK
UKHW022211230426
12048UKWH00016BA/773